THE ULTIMATE GUIDE TO:

COUPONING FOR THE BUSY WOMAN

BY:
JULIA CARTER

DEDICATION

I dedicate this book to my wonderful husband and children. You have all truly been a blessing in my life!

TABLE OF CONTENTS

INTRODUCTION

My couponing journey began in 2020. As a stay-at home mom with a family of six at the time, being unemployed and on one income, I asked the Lord to give me wisdom on how to help my husband save money. After scrolling through Facebook, I stumbled across a picture of stockpiled diapers. That got my immediate attention. Being a mother of four, now five, I had one child in diapers and another in pull-ups, and we all know how expensive diapers are. I began to research and watch various YouTube videos on the subject.

After learning the basics, I made my first couponing trip. I had developed a little bit of knowledge, and now it was time to put it to use.

Couponing is one of those things where you learn and grow as you go. I stocked up on all the necessities: toothpaste, tissue, detergent; the basics. I was on a roll. Then, bam, the pandemic hit. Tissue began to be cleared from the shelves and became as rare as fine gold, but I was not worried. Why? I had an abundant supply because God had given me wisdom on how to coupon. By the time I got to my last pack tissue appeared on the shelves again. God carried my family through with the wisdom He had given me, preparing us for things only He could see.

In times like these, when inflation is at an all-time high, saving money is crucial. If we can save in a few areas, we can have the extra money needed for groceries or other things. Let this book be your guide to help you master couponing, save money, and beat inflation.

Your Why

Before we get into the good stuff, we must address one important thing: your why. Why do you want to coupon? When it comes to couponing, there are good days, and there are bad days. Things do not always go according to plan. You may spend time coming up with deals, head to the store, and find an item on your list is not in stock. That can be frustrating as you have to rethink your scenario and find an item to replace the out-of-stock item. You may also deal with other things such as rewards not printing or not-so coupon-friendly cashiers. But do not get discouraged because the good days far outweigh the bad, and the benefits of couponing are very rewarding.

Your "why" is your anchor. It keeps you from giving up on those bad days. Maybe you want to start couponing simply to save money, or you are a stay-at-home mom and a one-income family like my household. Whatever your why may be, please keep it in the back of your mind for the discouraging days because planned outcomes do not always materialize. Nevertheless, couponing is fun and rewarding, allowing you to try new products at a very low cost or even free. And who does not like free?

CHAPTER ONE:
THE FOUNDATION

Couponing aims to get your total down to ***the rock-bottom price***

This chapter will discuss the rules and foundational information that every couponer MUST know. This information will teach you how to read a coupon, use a coupon, and avoid coupon fraud. We want to be sure we are abiding by the rules as well as abiding by the law. Couponing aims to get your total down to the **rock-bottom price**. Rock-bottom price means you cannot get the product any cheaper.

This would also be considered a **stock-up price.** Stock-up price is when the price of an item is so low you want to stock up on that item. Please remember that coupon deals change every Sunday and last until the following Saturday. These deals are also cyclical; they come back around every six weeks. Whatever product you are stocking up on, stock up enough to last your household six weeks until the deal rolls around again. This will help you build a nice stockpile that suits your family.

The Four Main Coupon Suppliers

There are typically three coupon inserts found in the local Sunday newspaper. SmartSource (SS), Save, and Unilever. These coupon inserts will vary each week. One week you may get a SmartSource and Save insert; another week, you may get SmartSource, Save, and Unilever. You can check to see what inserts will come that week and what coupons will be in those inserts by simply searching 'Sunday inserts preview' on

Google. These inserts are also regional, meaning that not every state will receive them in their Sunday papers.

The coupons contained in the SmartSource and Save are not brand specific; they will have various coupons for various products. However, the coupons found in Unilever are brand-specific for the items they make. Coupons such as Dove, Axe, and Vaseline coupons will be found in the Unilever insert.

Another coupon manufacturer is Proctor and Gamble (P&G). This manufacturer no longer provides coupon inserts. However, they provide printable coupons on their website, www.pggoodeveryday.com. These coupons are also brand-specific. Proctor and Gamble produce tons of products, from Tide to Pampers, Olay, and Crest. These are the products you will find coupons for, among other products, on their website.

Paper, Printable, And Digital Coupons

In this section, we will discuss the different forms of coupons. The various forms include paper, printable, and digital. We will also discuss where you will find each type of coupon based on the form you are looking for.

Paper (or insert) coupons:

Back in the day, this was the normal way of couponing, and is still popular today. This type of coupon requires finding the coupons, cutting the coupons, and keeping up with expiration dates.

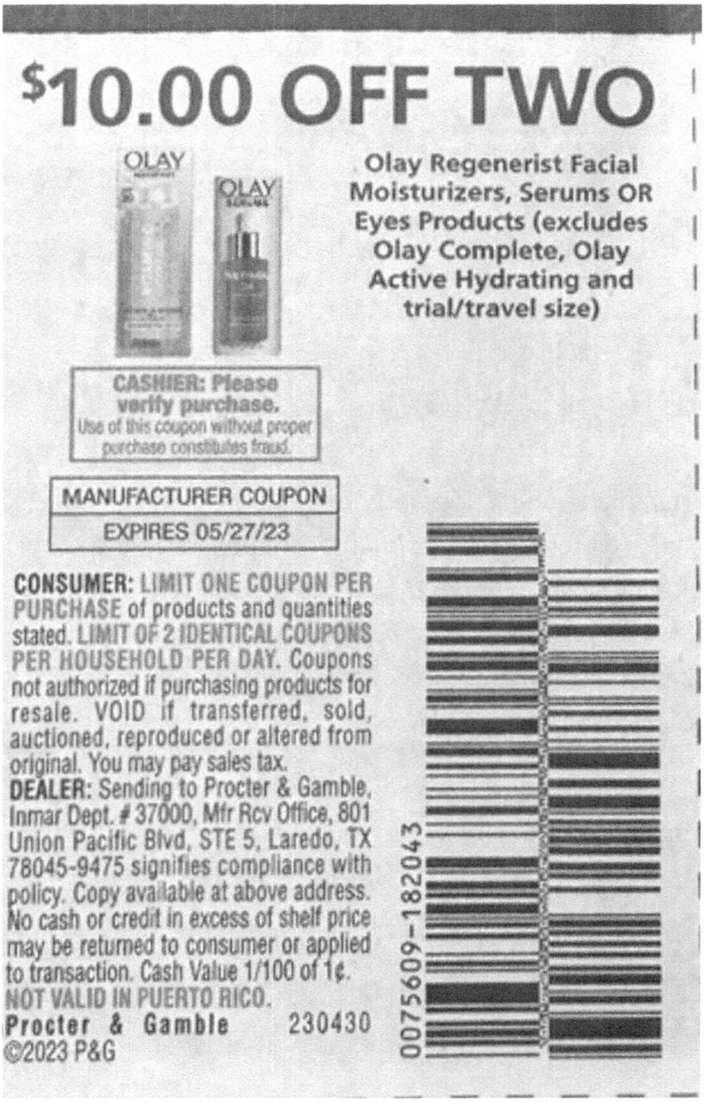

It is always a good idea to have paper coupons because not all stores have digital in-app coupons. Paper coupons allow you to use them at any store that accepts them. As mentioned, paper coupons can be found in your local Sunday newspaper. If you live in a region that does not receive newspaper inserts, you may order inserts online at websites like Bq Savings and www.sundayinserts.com.

Printable Coupons:

Printable coupons typically operate the same as paper coupons. The only difference is printable coupons require a printer for printing and usually have a next-day expiration. Normally, you are allowed one print per coupon. If you plan to print coupons for your coupon trip print them just before you head to the store to avoid the coupon expiring before use.

Digital Coupons:

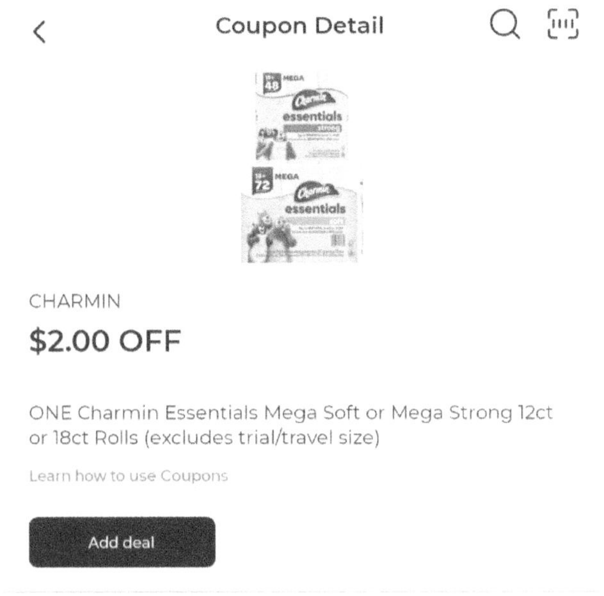

Digital coupons have now become the most popular type of coupon. These coupons are the easiest to find and maintain. Digital coupons are in-app, meaning you can find them in the stores' app. All digital coupons are of a one-time use and will disappear from your app coupon section after the coupon has been used. These coupons typically have a week to be used before they expire. They change weekly and are cyclical with the deals. Digital coupons must be clipped to your account in the coupon section of the app to apply at checkout.

Manufacturer Coupons Vs. Store Coupons

There are two kinds of coupons: manufacturer coupons and store coupons. Whether the coupon is paper, printed, or digital, it will fall into one of these categories. Knowing the difference will help you use the coupon successfully.

Manufacturer Coupons:

Manufacturer coupons come from the manufacturer of the coupon product. They are not store-specific and can be used anywhere coupons are accepted. After the use of the coupon, the manufacturer reimburses the store cash for the value of the coupon.

This is why it is super important that you use the coupon on the product it is intended for. When you use a coupon on a product it is not intended for not only is it coupon fraud but the company will not be reimbursed for that coupon. It causes the store to lose money, forcing them to crack down on couponing, change their coupon policy, or disallow coupon usage.

Store Coupons:

Store coupons are store-specific coupons that the store gives for that store. For example, if I have a Walgreens store coupon, I cannot use that coupon at CVS. I must use that coupon at Walgreens. These coupons will most likely be found in the store's app, on their website, or printed from their Catalina machine.

Stacking Both Store And Manufacturer Coupons

Stacking is a term used to describe the ability to use more than one coupon on one item. You can only use one manufacturer coupon per item and one store coupon per item. When it comes to stacking, you can use one manufacturer coupon and one store coupon simultaneously on one item.

How To Read And Understand Coupons

If we closely examine the coupon above, it begins with the value of the coupon. Beneath, it details what the coupon can be used for and what it excludes. The coupon also shows us the type of coupon.

In this case, it is a manufacturer coupon, and the expiration date is listed.

Next, we have information directed to the consumer and the dealer. We will focus on the consumer portion since that is where we come into play during the transaction. The coupon states to 'limit one coupon per purchase of products and quantities stated. Limit of 4 identical coupons per household per day'. What this means is you may only use one coupon per item (purchase), and you may only use four of the same coupons in one transaction. For example, if I buy four packs of Pampers I can use one manufacturer coupon per pack that I am purchasing, but the coupon also states that I have a limit of four IDENTICAL coupons I can use daily.

I emphasized identical because a digital coupon and a printable coupon are not identical to an insert coupon like the one above. Even if the one I print looks exactly like my insert coupon it is still not identical.

They must be in the same form: insert, digital, or printable, to be counted as an identical coupon. Therefore, I can add a fifth pack in the same transaction and use a printable coupon on that fifth pack if I choose.

Store Policies

Regarding store policies, each store has its own coupon policy. It is wise to look up this information and become familiar with it. You do not have to read the entire store policy, just the part about couponing. This will help you adhere to the store's rules and know your rights as a couponer.

Now that we have a solid foundation laid in the basics, let the fun begin! In the next few chapters we will break down the specifics of the three main stores couponers shop at. The goal is to give you pro-level knowledge before you make your first couponing trip. Start by installing these three store apps onto your phone, Dollar General, Walgreens, and CVS, to access the in-app digital coupons and the weekly ads. You can now create an account in the app using your telephone number. At the checkout, you will type in your phone number on the pen pad and all clipped coupons will automatically apply to each qualifying product. The process is the same for each store.

CHAPTER TWO:
DOLLAR GENERAL

Dollar General is a very beginner-friendly store. It is easy to grasp and is a great place to start your couponing journey. In the world of couponing, Dollar General is best known for the $5 off $25 Saturdays.

This only takes place on Saturdays and gives you an additional $5 in savings when you spend at least $25. You may have seen these at the bottom of your Dollar General receipt but never paid much attention to it, like myself, before couponing.

$5 OFF $25

The picture above shows the paper version of the $5 off $25. It lists the Saturday that the coupon is valid for. At the bottom of the receipt, there will be a barcode that the cashier can scan to remove your additional five-dollar savings at the register. This coupon can also be clipped as a digital coupon in the Dollar General app. All $5 off $25, both paper and digital, coupons are of a one-time use.

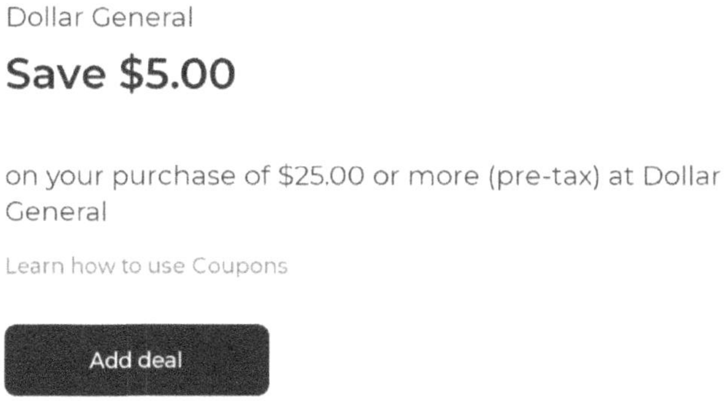

This is the digital version of the $5 off $25 and can be found in the 'delas' section of the Dollar General app. Be sure to click the 'Add deal' button to ensure the coupon is clipped to your account and all other coupons you want to add.

Upon entering your phone number at the register, this coupon will stack with any additional coupons for qualifying products in your transaction.

Instant Savings

Instant savings are savings that are instantly deducted.

For example, the picture above states that you will instantly save $2 for spending $8 on Dove, Suave, Tresemme, Axe, Degree, and Caress products. This means that once you meet the minimum requirements of $8, your instant savings of $2 will come off at checkout; no coupons needed, no account needed. It is a store promotion.

Applying this to a coupon scenario means that this additional $2 will come off and stack with any other coupons you have for those qualifying instant savings products. You do not have to stick to one brand; you can mix and match products on this deal.

If we add this to a $5 off $25 Saturday scenario, you must remember that any instant savings will automatically be deducted from your $25 requirement. For instance, if all the products in your cart total $25 and you did the $2 instant savings deal mentioned above, your $25 total now drops to $23, putting you under your $25 requirement. In this case, you would want to build your transaction up to $27 so when the $2 instant savings is applied, you are still at your $25 requirement for your $5 off $25 savings.

Weekly Ad

The weekly ad for Dollar General can be found in paper form in the store or digital form in the app. This is a useful resource for planning. It tells you the items on sale and the savings after applying the digital coupon. These help you know what to expect regarding what your total should be after coupons are applied.

Always know your total after-tax before going to the register. Find out the sales tax rate in your state and add this to your total before deducting any coupons. Calculate all products in your cart, multiply the sales tax percentage, and then subtract all coupons. This will give you the total of the transaction after tax. This is a safety measure in case something goes wrong as far as a coupon not applying at check out. This enables you to pinpoint what went wrong and fix it. Do not be afraid to cancel a transaction if it is not the expected total.

That is the reason for couponing; to save money. Never pay for a transaction that is over your expected total. ***You will feel better walking out with your money instead of paying for a transaction that is over what you anticipated.***

Apologize and let the cashier know it is not the total you expected. Ask the cashier which coupons came off. This will tell you if a coupon did not come off. Cancel the transaction, step away, and figure out what went wrong. Make sure all coupons are clipped, recalculate your total and try the transaction again.

Another way to avoid issues is always to remember to scan your items in the app. When you scan your items, the coupons that will attach to that item will show. This helps to ensure the product qualifies for the coupon.

How To Do A Deal At Dollar General

Now that we have learned the foundation for couponing at Dollar General I will show you how to do a $5 off $25 spend deal. A spend deal is a deal that requires you to spend a certain amount of money, known as a spend requirement, in order to receive something. In this case it will be an additional $5 off with a spend requirement of $25. We must build our transaction up to $25 and pair it with our coupons. Easy right? Let's start with this $5 off $15 deal.

Coupon Detail

DG Store Coupon

Dollar General

$5.00 OFF PURCHASE OF $15.00

Any all® Snuggle® Purex® Purex Crystals® Persil® Products When You Spend $15.00 or More

Notice that this is a Dollar General store coupon. This tells us that this coupon will **stack,** meaning, you will also be able to use manufacturer coupons for qualifying products with this discount. In this case, we will receive an additional $5 off when we spend $15 on All, Snuggle, Purex, Purex Crystals, or Persil products. We will pair this deal with our $5 off $25 scenario.

The first product we could add to our cart is this Persil for $10.95. Notice the price tag says 'DG Digital Coupon.' When you see this on a Dollar General sales tag it means there is a digital in-app coupon for that product. In this case, we have a $2 digital coupon for this product. This product qualifies for the $15 spend deal mentioned above leaving us with $4.05 left to meet that requirement.

Snuggle is another qualifying product. Once again we see the 'DG Digital Coupon' on the sales tag. There is a $1.25 in-app coupon for this item. The product is $3.75, leaving us with only $0.30 needed to meet our spend $15 requirement.

Our final spend $15 deal item is another bottle of Snuggle for $3.75. There is no coupon for this item since we have used our $1.25 coupon for the other bottle, bringing our total to $18.45. We now qualify for the additional $5 off for spending $15 on these products. Remember, we are incorporating this deal into our spend $25 scenario to qualify for another $5 off. This is why our total for the $15 scenario is slightly higher than $15. This will help us reach our $25 amount for the $5 off $25.

Coupon Detail

BIC® Razors

Save $3.00

on the purchase of ANY ONE (1) BIC® Soleil®, BIC® Flex™, BIC® EasyRinse™, or BIC® Comfort 3 Hybrid®/ Refillable Disposable Razor pack (excludes Soleil® Simply Smooth™ 3 pack & trial and travel sizes)

Learn how to use Coupons

Add deal

Bic Soleil Sensitive Women'S 3-Blade Disposable Razor, Lubricating Strip With Vitamin E And Aloe, 3-Count

0.0 out of 5 stars

$7.00

Deals available

Our final product for our $5 off $25 scenario are these Bic razors for $7.00 with a $3.00 off coupon. This brings our final total with the Persil and Snuggle included to $25.45. We have met our spend requirement to get another $5 off for spending $25. After our $5 for spending $25 comes off, our $5 for spending $15 on Persil and Snuggle comes off, as well as our $2.00 for the Persil, the $1.25 for the Snuggle, and the $3.00 for the Bic razor, our final total for all of these products is just $9.20.

That is less than our most expensive item, the Persil, for $10.95. This a great stock-up price. If you have other family members in the home who can create a Dollar General account you can do this deal more than once to begin building your stockpile. Remember, the $5 off $25 is for Saturdays only. Any deal you do during the week will not have the additional $5 off. You can do cheap deals throughout the week but depending on the deal you can usually get them cheaper by waiting until Saturday.

CHAPTER THREE: WALGREENS

Walgreens is a store that is a bit more complicated but with the guidance in this book you will master it in no time. Once again, you want to download the app and create an account to access the digital coupons and weekly ads. This is a fun and rewarding store to coupon at with many benefits and amazing savings on all the name-brand products you love.

Store Rewards

Let us start by discussing the different store rewards at Walgreens. There are two different forms of store rewards that you will earn for doing certain deals: Walgreens cash and register rewards. We will go into specific details about each of these rewards.

Walgreens Cash:

Walgreens cash is store money, or Walgreens store currency, that you can use to purchase just about anything in the store. You earn it by making transactions that are giving back Walgreens cash for purchasing certain products. You will automatically earn 1% Walgreens cash back on all transactions and 5% back on Walgreens branded products. Having Walgreens cash is similar to having a bank account. It is stored in your Walgreens account and can be used when checking out.

You can check your Walgreens cash balance by looking on the app's home page. However, there is a catch when it comes to using it. Walgreens cash can only be spent in certain increments: $1, $2, $3, $4, $5, then it jumps to $10, $20, and then jumps up to $50, which is the maximum amount you can spend per day.

For example, if I did a transaction totaling $2, I could use $2 in Walgreens cash and then pay the tax out of pocket. If I had a transaction that totaled $8, I could use $5 in Walgreens cash and pay the $3 plus tax out of pocket. I cannot use $8 in Walgreens cash since the next amount I can use is $10. I would have to add more items to my transaction, build my transaction up to $10, use $10 in Walgreens cash, and pay the tax; paying less out-of-pocket. This is one of the benefits of building up your Walgreens cash.

The goal of couponing is to spend as little out of pocket as possible and having store money allows you to do just that.

Register Rewards:

Register rewards are the paper form of Walgreens store currency. It is similar to having physical cash in hand to be used in the store. **Only ONE register reward will print per deal.**

For example, if the deal is buy two boxes of Crest toothpaste and receive a $4 register reward and I buy four tubes of toothpaste only one register reward will print.

I will not get two register rewards for buying four tubes of toothpaste. One register reward will print per deal.

If the deal was giving back $4 in Walgreens cash, I could grab four toothpastes and get back $8 in Walgreens cash. Walgreens cash will double, but register rewards will not. **We use register rewards to help lower our out-of-pocket costs.** Register rewards are not account-specific, meaning you can use them on any account with any transaction except certain products such as alcohol, tobacco products, and prescriptions.

These reward amounts vary by deal and there are two types of register rewards: manufacturer and store register rewards. We must go over the difference between the two.

Manufacturer Register Rewards:

If you notice, at the top of the reward, it tells us what type of register reward it is and the expiration date. These types of register rewards operate the same as a regular manufacturer coupon. These rewards do not lower. If the register reward has a value of $4, your total must be a minimum of $4. You can use these to help reduce your out-of-pocket costs. There is no limit to how many manufacturer register rewards you can use in one transaction.

Store Coupon Register Rewards:

You will notice at the top of this reward it is a store coupon. Although they operate the same as the manufacturer register rewards, these are store discounts, similar to the instant savings discussed in the Dollar

General chapter. The major difference is you can only use one per transaction, regardless of **filler items,** a cheap item needed to reach a spend requirement, because it is recognized in the system as a store discount. When doing a spend deal this kind of register reward will reduce your total just like the instant savings at Dollar General.

For example, if you have a spend booster of $20 get back $5 in Walgreens cash and you want to use this $4 register reward, you will build the transaction up to $24 to meet your $20 spend requirement. Similar to the instant savings at Dollar General. If you are not doing a spend deal with a spend requirement you can use this reward on anything you want in the store.

Walgreens Store Coupon:

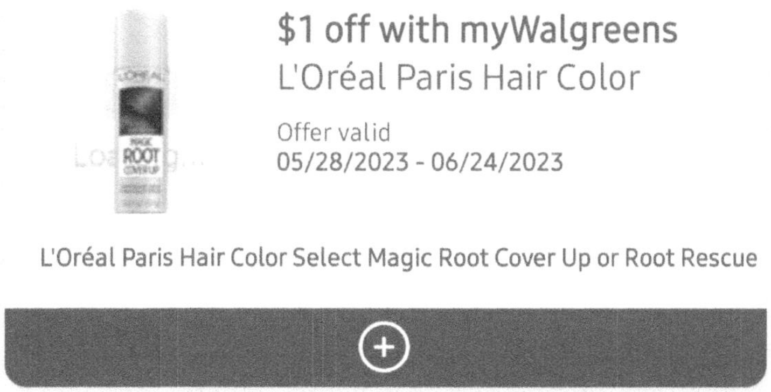

Here we have another example of a Walgreens store coupon. Any in-app digital coupon with the 'my Walgreens' on it will act the same as a store register reward. Coupons of this sort are considered as store discounts and will drop your total below any spend requirement.

You can also see the plus sign on the coupon. That is what you must click to clip the coupon to your account. You will also be able to see any products attached to this particular coupon. You will also see this when you scan any of the products in the store. Again, you want to scan your items to ensure the coupon you want to use attaches to the product.

Spend Boosters:

Spend boosters are boosters with spend requirements that give you rewards, specifically Walgreens cash, for spending a certain amount of money. These vary by account, change weekly, are of one-time use, and come in digital and paper forms. When using a spend booster, it is important to note that you CANNOT use Walgreens cash to pay for these transactions without knowing how to do so. There are necessary steps that must be taken in order to pay with Walgreens cash and still receive your Walgreens cash. We will discuss this later in the chapter.

Paper Boosters:

Paper boosters are rewards printed from the store's **Catalina machine**. The Catalina machine behind the cash register prints out various things upon checkout including register rewards. These spend boosters print randomly and can be used on your next transaction. The amount of these rewards are also random. You may get one that is $5 when you spend $22 or $10 when you spend $50. Normally, you have a week before these expire and you may only use one paper booster per transaction.

Digital Booster:

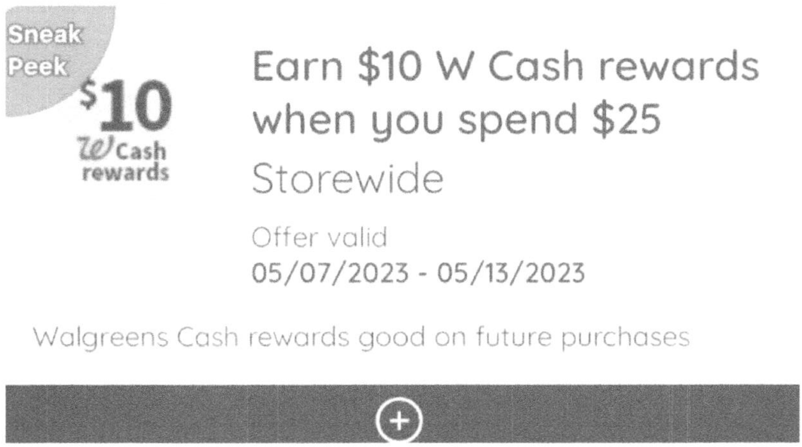

The digital booster is in-app in the coupon section. This booster must be clipped to your account to receive the Walgreens cash. These vary by account, change weekly, and are of one-time use as well. You may simultaneously use a digital and paper spend booster on the same transaction.

When doing this, you **must** meet the higher spend amount. For example, if I had a spend $25 to get $10 digital booster and the paper booster above of spend $35 get back $7, I must pay $35 to receive the $10 and the $7 since $35 is the higher amount of both the boosters. Use these spend boosters and your coupons for maximum savings and to build your store money. You want to use store money on deals that will give you back store money paired with the digital and paper spend boosters.

Walgreens Sales Tags

It is important to know how to read Walgreens sales tags. This will help you understand what products are included in the deal, how much you must spend to receive the reward, which type of reward you will receive, and how much the reward will be. If the deal is giving back

Walgreens cash, it will automatically deposit into your Walgreens account. If the deal is giving back a register reward it will be printed from the Catalina machine once you pay for your transaction.

Walgreens Cash Sales Tag:

This Walgreens tag tells us that we will receive $5 in Walgreens cash for spending $15 on participating Nivea products. This $15 must be met before any coupons are applied. For example, let's say I find two bottles of Nivea lotion priced at $10.99, And they are also part of the buy one get one 50% off deal. That would be $10.99 for the first bottle and $5.50 for the second bottle, for a total cost of $16.49.

I also have two coupons for these products: $3 off and $2 off. After these coupons are applied, my total drops down to $11.49. I would still receive my $5 in Walgreens cash because the spend requirement was met before the coupons were applied.

It is also important to know that **if a spend deal is giving back Walgreens cash, like this one, you cannot use Walgreens cash to pay.** If this Nivea spend deal was giving back a $5 register reward we could use Walgreens cash to pay and still receive our register reward. Any time the tag says 'spend' and is giving back Walgreens cash you cannot pay with Walgreens cash and still receive the Walgreens cash. To find out which Nivea products are included in this deal, you would use the in-app scanner to see if the deal and coupon are attaching to that Nivea product.

Upon scanning the product the "spend $15 on participating" Nivea products will appear. If it does not appear that particular item is not included in this deal. Make the in-app scanner your best couponing buddy to avoid mistakes at the counter. If any coupons are attached to that specific item they will also show. After meeting the $15 spend amount the $5 Walgreens cash will automatically be deposited in your Walgreens account to be used on your next transaction.

The sales tag also tells us how long a deal will last. We are given the date the deal ends in the lower right-hand corner. Looking at the dates on the tag will tell you if the deal is a month-long deal or just for that week.

Register Reward Sales Tag:

Here we have another deal on personal care products. When we spend $20 on participating products we will receive a $5 register reward. Usually the tag will list the specific brands that are included in the deals. A personal care deal usually includes body wash, hair care, oral care, and diapers. If the specific brands are not listed on the sales tag like this one you can look in the in-app weekly ad to see which products are included. This deal type is usually called the 'Deals of the Week' promotion. It is important to remember never to do two of these deals in one transaction when receiving a registered reward and are part of the same promotion.

For example, if the deal has buy two Dove body washes at $7 and get back a $5 register reward, and they also have Huggies on sale for buy two at $21 get back a $5 register reward; if they are both included in the 'Deals of the week' promotion you will not get two register rewards for buying both the Dove body wash and the Huggies diapers in the same transaction because they are part of the same weekly promotion.

You must do these deals separately to receive the register reward for both deals. However, suppose Dove is giving back a $5 register reward, and Huggies is giving back a $4 register reward. In that case, although they are part of the 'Deals of the Week' promotion, you will receive both register rewards because they are separate deals giving a different amount of reward. The tags and ad will specify which brands are included in that deal.

Only For You Coupons:

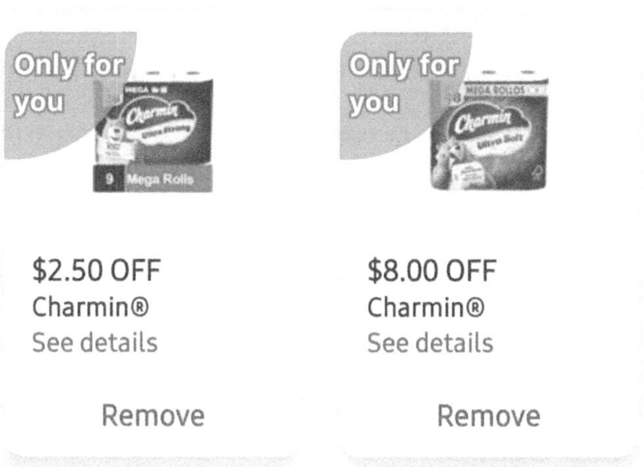

It is important to know how coupons apply. If you have two coupons for the same product, the lower-value coupon will attach to the product before the higher-value coupon. This applies to all stores. However, there are some exceptions.

Digital coupons with the 'only for you' in the left-hand corner are only for you. Some accounts may get them, while others may not. If an 'only for you' coupon is clipped to your account it will

ALWAYS attach before any other digital coupon regardless of the amount of other clipped coupons for that product.

For example, if I have both 'only for you' Charmin coupons in my app and grab one pack of Charmin, the $8 coupon will attach first. However, if these were not 'only for you' coupons, the $2.50 coupon would attach first. Your "only for you" coupons will always attach first with the higher value attaching before the lower value. You would not need to remove the lower-value coupon for the higher-value coupon to apply.

Now, let's say the $8.00 "only for you" coupon and the $2.50 "only for you" coupon is attaching to the red pack of Charmin, but only the $2.50 coupon is attaching to the blue pack. You would want to buy one red and one blue. When checking out, you would have the cashier scan the red pack first to guarantee the $8.00 coupon attaches to it, leaving the $2.50 coupon to attach to the blue pack.

Remember, with "only for you" coupons, the highest-value coupon attaches first. If the cashier were to scan the blue pack first, the $8.00 coupon would attach to that pack, but the $2.50 coupon would not attach to the red pack, making your total $2.50 higher. Again, using the in-app scanner you can always check if a coupon attaches to an item.

How To Use Walgreens Cash And Register Rewards On A Spend Deal

Using Walgreens cash to pay for your transactions greatly reduces your out-of-pocket cost to very low totals or, often, just paying taxes. This is expert couponing knowledge and may be hard to grasp at first. Still, as you begin couponing at Walgreens you will be able to understand the information in this section as you become familiar with everything we have discussed in this chapter. If you are new to couponing at Walgreens I suggest becoming familiar with the basics before attempting to understand this information. However, if you are ready to achieve maximum savings at Walgreens with little pay out-of-pocket keep reading.

Before we get into the topic, knowing how Walgreens' system operates is important. Walgreens system recognizes **manufacturer** register rewards and manufacturer coupons, **NOT** store register rewards or store coupons, as cash. For example, a $5 manufacturer register reward is recognized in the system the same way the system would recognize a $5 bill. This also applies to manufacturer coupons. A $2 manufacturer coupon for Colgate toothpaste would be recognized as $2 "cash" in the system regardless of the coupon product's brand or the coupon's value. This applies to digital, paper, and printable coupons and manufacturer register rewards; it does not apply to store register rewards or store coupons.

As I mentioned, you will receive an in-app digital spend booster every week in your Walgreens app. For this scenario, we will use the spend booster pictured below.

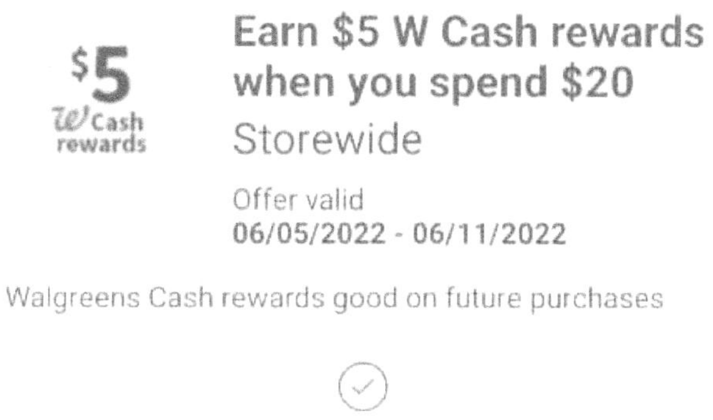

In this case, we must spend $20 to earn $5 in Walgreens cash. The goal is to have our **manufacturer** coupons, and any **manufacturer** register rewards pay for our $20 spend requirement. Let's say we have $20 Walgreens cash in our account and two $5 manufacturer register rewards from a previous transaction that we want to use to help lower our out-of-pocket cost. Remember, manufacturer register rewards, manufacturer coupons, cash, and debit/credit card payments are recognized as cash payments in the system. Walgreens cash is **NOT** recognized as a cash payment on a spend deal. This is why you cannot use Walgreens cash on a spend deal without taking certain precautions.

Returning to the scenario, we have two $5 manufacturer register rewards, which means we already have $10 towards our $20 spend requirement, which means we now only need ten more dollars. We will begin to build our transaction up to allow our manufacturer coupons to cover our spend total. Let's say we have this $5 Olay coupon we want to use.

This coupon gives us $5 off when we purchase three qualifying products. We now have $15, the two $5 register rewards and the $5 Olay coupon, that we can deduct from our spend requirement, leaving only $5 left to cover.

Now, this is where you will need to pay close attention. Our Olay coupon is $5 off three Olay body wash products. Olay body wash is also on sale for $7 per bottle in this scenario.

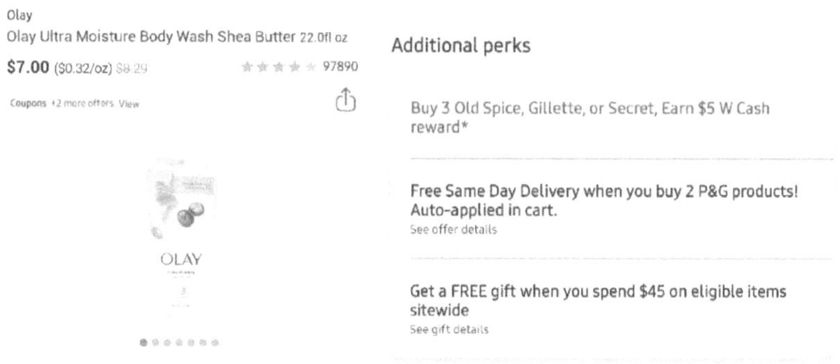

The picture on the right also says that we will receive $5 in Walgreens cash when we buy three Olay body washes. If we put three body washes in our cart, we would have a total of $21 in product. That means we have met our $20 spend requirement. We could head to the register to check out, type in our phone number, and give the cashier our two $5 register rewards leaving us to pay

$6.00 out of pocket. We would not be able to use Walgreens cash and still earn our Walgreens cash back for spending $20 because our $5 coupon and two $5 register rewards only totaled $15, leaving us with $5 still needed to meet the $20 requirement which we would need to pay with either cash or our debit/credit card. We would then receive $5 in Walgreens cash for spending $20 and our $5 register reward for buying three Olay body washes. The transaction would be free and a $4 **money-maker.** A money maker is when you earn back more than you spent out of pocket. So because we spent $6 out-of-pocket and received back $10 in store money we earned back the $6 we just paid as well as an additional $4. That is a pretty good deal but we can do even better. We will build our transaction up to allow our coupons and register rewards to cover our $20 spend requirement. Again, Walgreens system recognizes manufacturer coupons, and manufacturer registers rewards as cash paid. Always keep that in mind. For this scenario we could keep the three Olay body washes and we could add two packs of Pampers diapers.

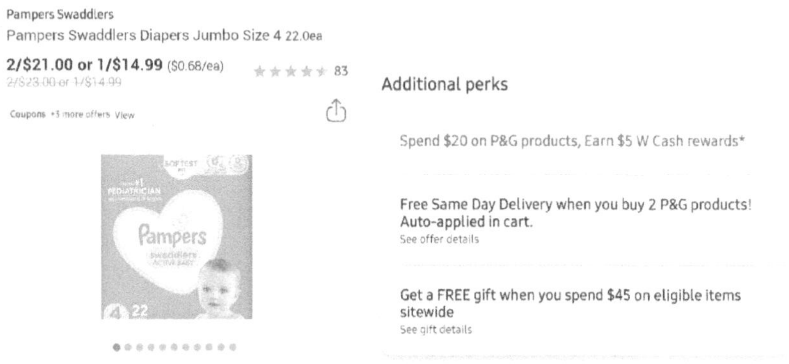

We see in the picture that Pampers are on sale for 2/$21. The image on the right tells us we will receive $5 Walgreens cash for spending $20 on P&G products. Pampers is a P&G product. We also have a $5 off two Pampers coupon.

Since we will purchase the $20 P&G spend requirement we will also receive another $5 in Walgreens cash for the Pampers. So we have the three Olay body washes in our cart and the two packs of Pampers diapers. That brings our total to $42. We have $10 in coupons, $5 for the Olay, $5 for the Pampers, and our two $5 manufacturer register rewards. That brings our total down to $22. Since we have allowed our coupons and manufacturer register rewards to cover our $20 spend requirement; the $5 Olay coupon, the $5 Pampers coupon, and the two $5 register rewards, we are free to use $20 in Walgreens cash to bring the balance even lower because our spend requirement has been met via coupons and register rewards. Our final cost for all these items will be $2, or just forty cents per item. WOW!

After we pay for our transaction, we will receive $15 back in Walgreens cash: $5 for buying three Olay body washes, $5 for

for spending $20 on P&G products, and our spend booster of $5 for spending $20. In this example you can see the true value in couponing. Forty cents per bag of diapers is amazing!

If you are doing a spend deal and are using a **paper** spend booster, and want to use Walgreens cash to pay, you **must** pay via contactless pay.

To add your payment method, go to the app and click the icon in the top right corner. Select 'personal information' then 'payment methods' to add a debit card. After adding your debit card, you will see a red "pay now" button on the home screen under 'wallet'. Select the 'manage payment and rewards' option. From there you can select the amount of Walgreens cash you would like to use. After you have selected the amount of Walgreens cash, you will select "pay now" and have the cashier scan the barcode on your phone. The payment and the Walgreens cash will come off automatically. You do not need to type your number in. The barcode will have all your account information as well as your coupons. Always know your total after tax, after coupons, and after any register rewards before checking out. **No surprises at the register**. If you do not use contactless pay when using a paper spend booster on a spend deal, you will not receive your Walgreens cash back for the spend booster.

This is the benefit of using Walgreens cash on a spend deal. We can have lower out-of-pocket costs and bigger money-makers.

If you have a situation where your coupon does not apply, or you did not receive your Walgreens cash, call customer service. They will check your transaction over the phone to see if you met the requirements to receive the reward and add it to your Walgreens cash account. If you have a situation where a register reward did not print, you will have to contact the Catalina company online, fill out the form, and they will mail you the register reward.

I hope I have made this as easy as possible for you to understand. Experience will bring expertise in this area. Again, if you are new to couponing get familiar with the basics at Walgreens before attempting to use Walgreens cash on a spend deal. You can always come back to this section of the book for any guidance you may need.

CHAPTER FOUR:
CVS

CVS is another popular store for couponing in the Couponing world. This store is similar to Walgreens whereby you earn rewards back for doing deals but there are major differences between the two stores; CVS is the least complicated. Again, download the CVS app and create an account using your phone number. After you create your account, you will receive an in-app ExtraCare card assigned to your phone number and email address. You may get a physical card in the store if you prefer. Now, let's discuss how to master couponing at CVS and maximize your savings.

CarePass

When you begin couponing at CVS, you will be given the option to sign up for Care Pass. This is done in the store at the register. Upon signing up, you will receive a free $10 ExtraCare buck that can be used immediately. Afterward there is a $5 monthly charge or $48 for the whole year to continue getting the $10 ExtraCare buck each month.

Whichever debit/credit card you sign up with is the card that will be charged monthly if that is the option you choose. This is voluntary and not essential to shopping at CVS, but it is a great resource if you plan to be a frequent couponer at this store.

ExtraBucks

ExtraBuck is the name of the rewards, or CVS store currency, you will receive for doing deals that are giving back ExtraBucks. When you have met the deal requirements, your ExtraBucks will print at the bottom of your receipt.

If you examine the picture, there is an expiration date. At the bottom of the ExtraBuck, you will notice it says 'ExtraCare Card #'. These ExtraBucks are account-specific. You can only use the ExtraBucks on the account you received the ExtraBucks on. This applies to both paper and digital.

ExtraBucks also come in digital form and can be clipped in the 'Deals & Rewards' section of the CVS app.

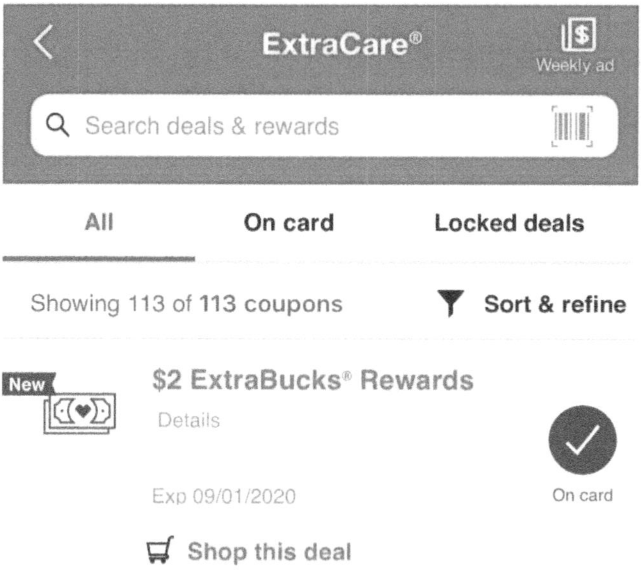

Once you clip the digital version, the paper version becomes void and can no longer be used. This also shows the expiration date and is a good option if you misplace the paper version or prefer to have it digitally.

Upon checking out, let the cashier know you want to use your ExtraBucks. No limit exists on how much ExtraBucks you can use in one transaction. One thing to remember when using them is to use the full amount. For instance, if I have this $2 ExtraBuck clipped to my account and my transaction total is $1, my $2 ExtraBuck will cover that one dollar, but I will lose the other $1 ExtraBuck. Get your total in products to $2 to use the full ExtraBuck reward and avoid losing the leftover amount.

CRTs (Cash Register Tape)

Cash register tape, most known as CRT, is an extra discount on certain products. Below, we see the digital form of a CRT.

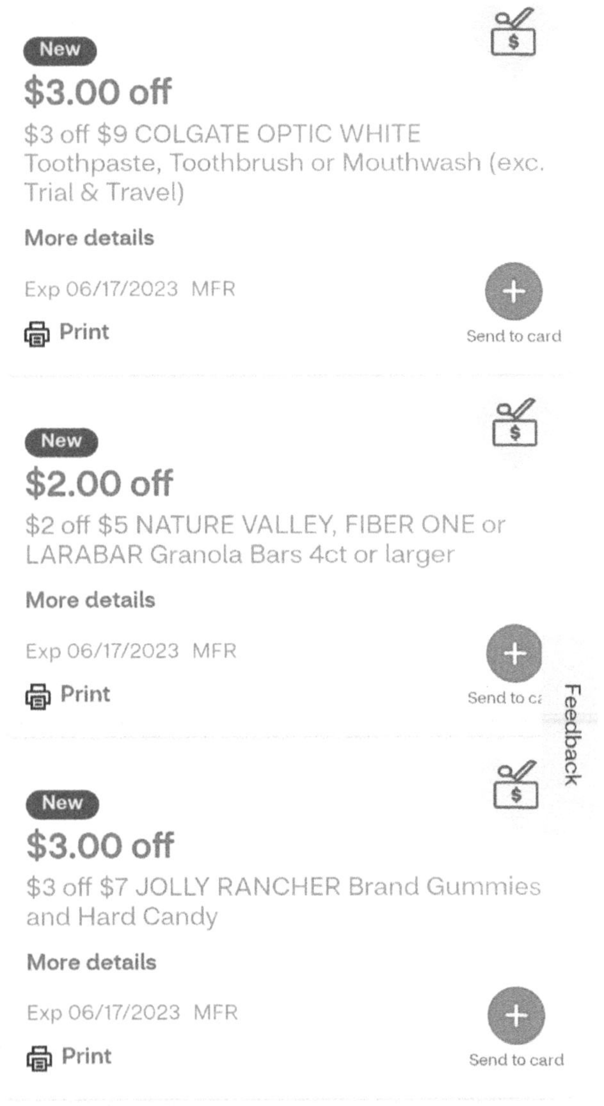

These are found in the app's 'Deals and Rewards' section. They are marked with a pink heart and scissors. CRTs vary by account and are based on the type of purchases you make. For example, if I buy diapers from CVS, I will begin to get diaper CRTs. The CRT may say, '$4 off when you spend $30 on Pampers diapers' or something along those lines. The amount will vary, and CRTs usually have a week to use before expiration.

Looking at the picture, if I often purchase Colgate toothpaste, Nature Valley bars, and Jolly Ranchers I will see CRT discounts in my CVS app for those products. CRTs will stack with coupons. For example, the $3 off $9 Colgate CRT will stack with a $1 Colgate coupon or whatever coupons I may have for Colgate products. When I meet the spend requirement of $9, an additional $3 will come off, along with the $1; giving me $4 in savings and receiving back the Extrabuck may come with this deal. Upon checking out the CRTs automatically appear when you type in your phone number. If you use self-checkout,they will come off once you click 'Finish and Pay'.

Another example would be the Venus Razor CRT.

We will receive an additional $10 off when we spend $20 on women's Venus Razors. The digital coupon on the right will stack with the CRT, giving me $13 in savings on qualifying Venus products.

Paper Crts And The Coupon Center

We previously discussed digital CRTs. Now we will discuss the paper CRTs and the red Coupon Center.

When you enter CVS you will find this red Coupon Center machine.

You can use this to check the price of items, or, you can use it to get the paper form of your CRTs. Whatever digital in-app CRTs you have on your account will print in paper form from this machine. Type in your phone number on the screen or scan your ExtraCare card via your phone or physical card to receive your CRTs. They operate the same as the digital form but with the paper form they must be scanned at checkout.

Examining the paper form we see the CRT will take an additional $3 off any Covergirl Cosmetics. In this case, there is no spend requirement which is the best type of CRT. You can pick out any Covergirl product, except trial and travel size, at any price and receive the $3 discount. Maximize your savings by pairing the CRT with a paper or digital Covergirl coupon for your chosen product.

We also see there is an expiration date as well as a scannable barcode. These are account-specific. The CRT ExtraCare card number must match the ExtraCare card account.

How To Read A CVS Price Tag

A CVS price tag tells us what we need to know about a deal. In the upper right corner of the yellow portion of the price tag is the deals expiration date. A typical CVS tag will have the dates the deal begins and when the deal ends. Below is the description of the deal and how much ExtraBucks we can expect to receive after we have met the deal's requirements. The picture on the right is a close-up of the bottom portion of the price tag. This portion tells us how many times we can do the deal. This deal has an offer limit of two per household per week. That means it is limited to two a week per household. If you attempt to do a deal more than the offer limit the ExtraBuck will not print.

How To Do A Deal At CVS

Now that we have covered the foundation of couponing at CVS, I want to give you a visual of how a deal is done using CRTs and paper/digital coupons.

CVS is popular with their weekly spend $30 get $10 ExtraBucks deal. This includes lots of various products. The deal consists of everything in the ad with the symbol shown in the blue circle. Wherever you see that symbol in the ad, the product is included in this spend $30 deal. You can mix and match any products that are included. We will now look at a scenario in this deal to see the savings you can get at CVS.

Notice the symbol we spoke of earlier on this Schick razor deal. It says we will receive a $10 ExtraBuck for spending $30 on any Schick, Edge, Skintimate, or Bulldog products. In the picture on the right at the top, we have a $3 off $10 Shick razor CRT. We also have a $4 Schick women's razor coupon at the bottom of the picture. Once again, these two will stack together if we meet the $10 spend requirement. Also notice the CRT is a manufacturer discount which means it will not drop our total as a store discount would. Now we will put together a Schick razor deal for our CVS scenario.

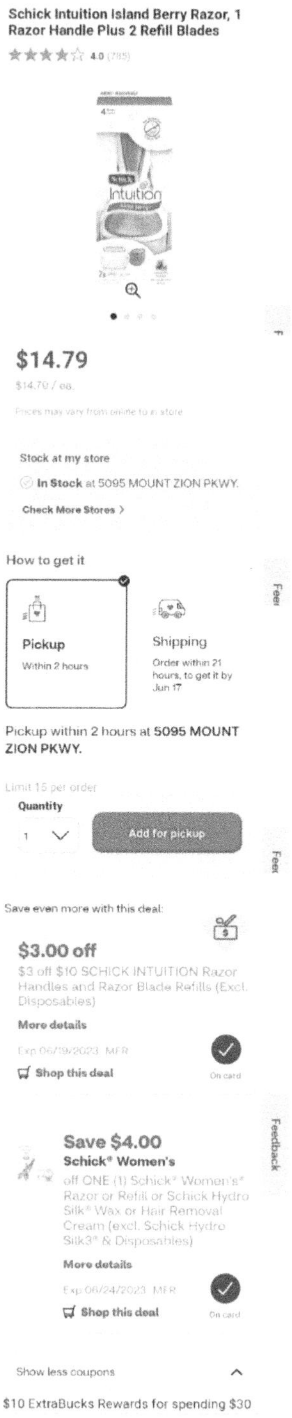
Schick Intuition Island Berry Razor, 1 Razor Handle Plus 2 Refill Blades
4.0
Intuition
$14.79
$14.79 / ea.
Prices may vary from online to in store
Stock at my store
In Stock at 5095 MOUNT ZION PKWY.
Check More Stores
How to get it
Pickup
Within 2 hours
Shipping
Order within 21 hours, to get it by Jun 17
Pickup within 2 hours at 5095 MOUNT ZION PKWY.
Limit 15 per order
Quantity
1
Add for pickup
Save even more with this deal:
$3.00 off
$3 off $10 SCHICK INTUITION Razor Handles and Razor Blade Refills (Excl. Disposables)
More details
Exp 06/19/2023 MFR
Shop this deal
On card
Save $4.00
Schick® Women's
off ONE (1) Schick® Women's® Razor or Refill or Schick Hydro Silk® Wax or Hair Removal Cream (excl. Schick Hydro Silk3® & Disposables)
More details
Exp 06/24/2023 MFR
Shop this deal
On card
Feedback
Show less coupons
$10 ExtraBucks Rewards for spending $30

Here we have a women's Schick Intuition razor priced at $14.79 that qualifies for the spend $30 deal. At the bottom we see our $3 off $10 CRT and our $4 Schick Women's digital coupon. This tells us that the CRT and the digital coupon will attach to this razor. You can check to see if the CRT and digital coupon are attaching by scanning the barcode on the razor or by selecting 'Shop this deal' at the bottom of the CRT and digital coupon. If the CRT and digital coupon are not attaching to the product they will not appear beneath the product like in the picture below.

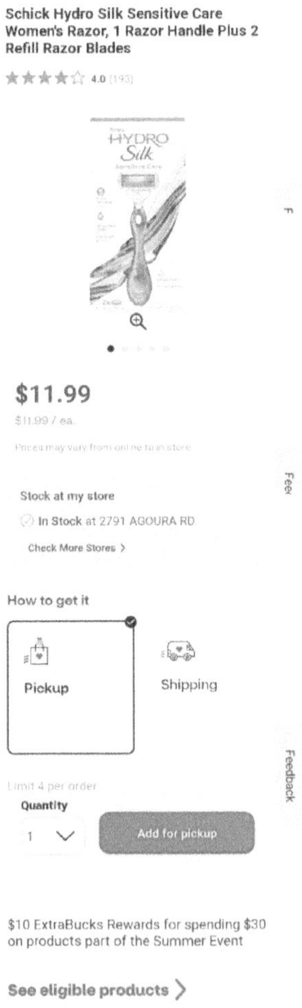

While this product qualifies for the spend $30 deal, our CRT and coupon will not attach to this razor.

Returning to our Schick deal scenario, we will add the women's Shick Intuition razor for $14.79 and this men's Shick razor for $11.99 with a $4 coupon.

To meet the rest of our $30 spend requirement we will add this Edge shaving cream for $3.99 that has a $1 off coupon.

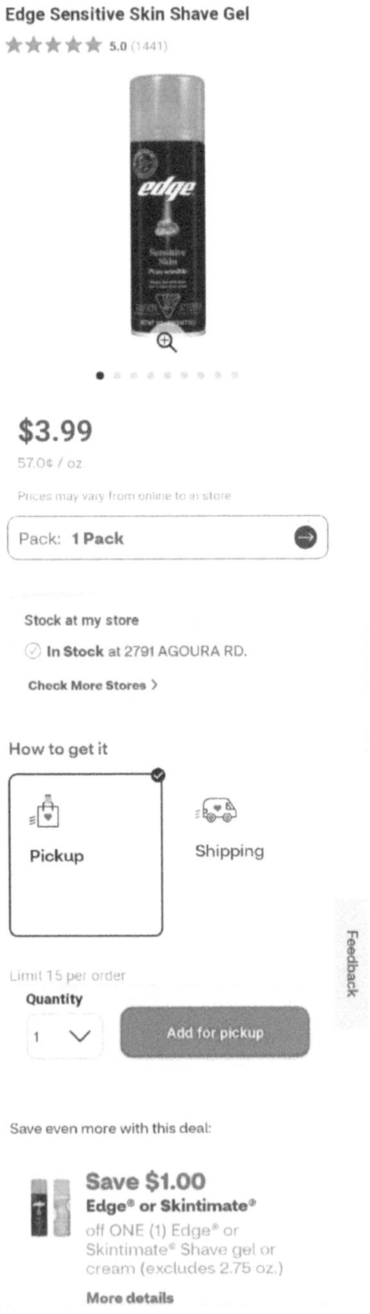

All these products qualify for the spend $30 deal. Our combined products cost $30.77 before coupons and taxes are applied. After our $3 off $10 Schick CRT and $9 in manufacturer coupons are applied, our total is $18.77. Remember, we are signing up for CarePass and receiving the free $10 ExtraBuck that we will use on this transaction to help lower our out-of-pocket cost. After applying the $10 ExtraBuck, our total is now $8.77. We will receive a $10 ExtraBuck for spending $30 on Shick and Edge products, making our final cost-free and a $1.23 money-maker. Now, I want to give you some important information about stacking multiple CRTs for products that are the same. For instance, say you have two of the same Venus CRTs pictured below in your account.

You would have to spend $40 to receive $20 off for both CRTs'. They will not stack in terms of you only paying $20 and receiving $20 off for both CRTs. You must combine the totals and spend the required amount for both CRTs combined to receive both discounts.

The 98% Rule And The Rewards Tracker

Most CVS stores have the 98% rule. If you are doing a spend requirement, you must meet at least 98% of that requirement to receive the ExtraBuck reward. For example, let's take the $30

Schick deal we did in the previous transaction. We would have needed at least $29.40 of the $30 to meet the spend requirement and still receive the $10 ExtraBuck. This applies to anything with a spend requirement at CVS. The Schick CRT

Stated that when we spend $10 on Shick products, we would receive $3 off. We would need to spend a minimum of $9.80 to receive the $3 discount.

With the rewards tracker, CVS tracks how much you have spent for any deal with a spend requirement for that week. If we had done the Shick deal above and only reached $25 of the $30 spend requirement and we paid the $25, the CVS rewards tracker will track that we have already spent $25 towards that spend $30 requirement.

We could return another day that week and purchase a qualifying product to reach the remaining $5 balance needed for the $30 spend requirement. That is just another amazing benefit of shopping at CVS. It helps when something may go wrong as far as a CRT or digital coupon not attaching. We would not have to attempt to reach the $30 again. The bottom of your receipt will show you how much you have tracked towards any spend deals. You will need to complete any incomplete spend deals that week since the deals start over each week.

CHAPTER FIVE:
REBATE APPS

Lastly, we will cover rebate apps. This is another way to maximize your savings and use apps to pay for your couponing trips without spending money from your personal bank account. There are many different rebate apps, but in this book, we will cover two of the most popular apps we use when couponing. Both apps can be downloaded from the app store on your device and only require an account to be made.

Ibotta

Ibotta is a rebate app that gives you cash back for purchasing certain products at certain stores. You can choose from many stores to see what the app is giving back on certain products. Ibotta offers cash back for all products, from food to personal care.

Here are a few examples of money back on food items at Walmart.

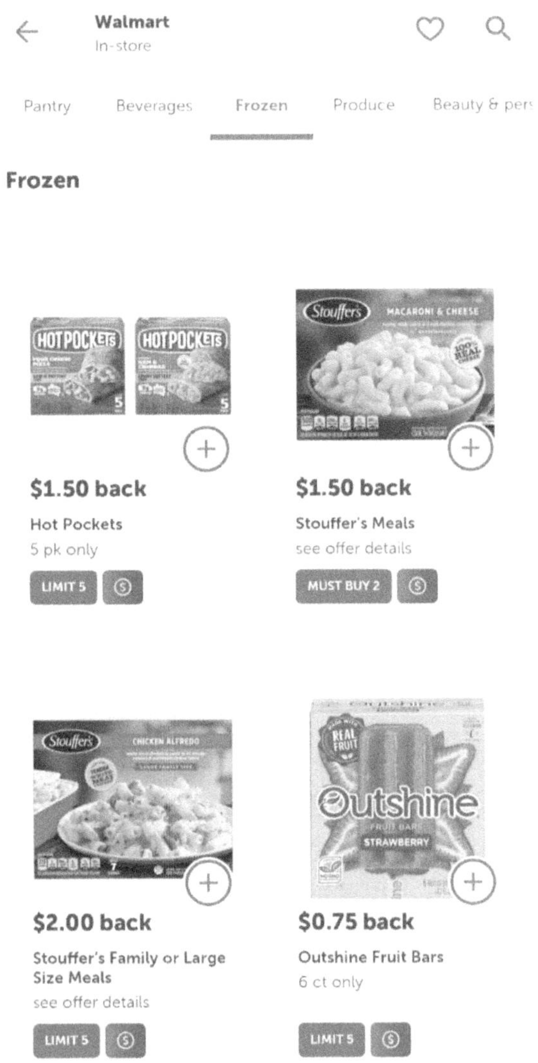

You will receive $1.50 back for purchasing the five-count box of Hot Pockets. Below, it tells us we have a limit of five. That means we can buy five boxes in one transaction and receive $1.50 back on each box. Some products, such as the Stouffers macaroni, require

you to purchase two boxes to receive the $1.50. These products change constantly, and receiving money back on products you are already buying is great.

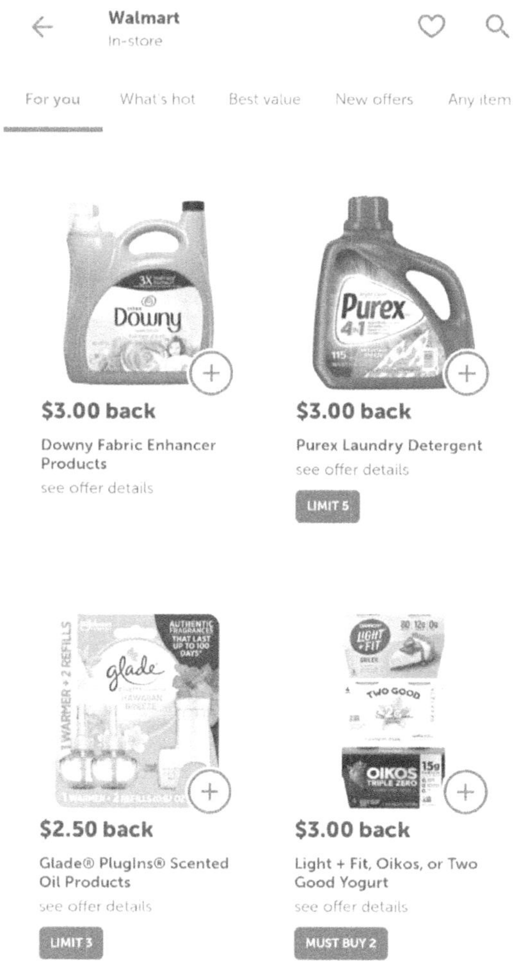

Again, we have laundry and other products that give cash back. All of these items can be paired with any coupons you may have. For example, if you have already purchased these items at Walgreens, you can select the store in the app and scan the receipt to receive the cash. For instance, if we take the Walgreens scenario we did in the Walgreens chapter, Ibotta would give us back $1.50 for each pack of diapers we purchased for up to five packs.

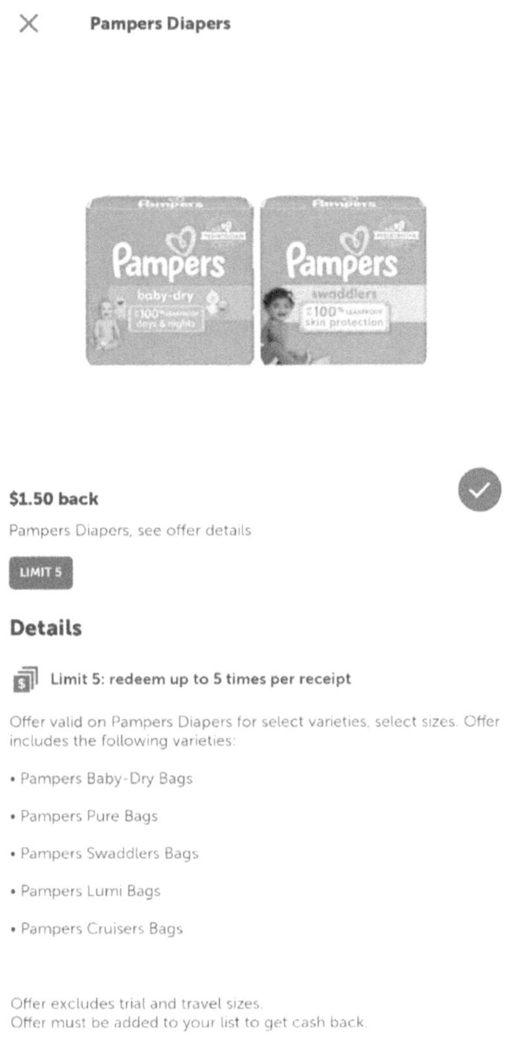

This makes our final Walgreens cost even lower.

Ibotta Bonuses:

Ibotta also gives additional cash-back bonuses for redeeming a certain amount of offers each week. For example, Starting Monday, Ibotta gives the “Midweek Money Maker” bonus.

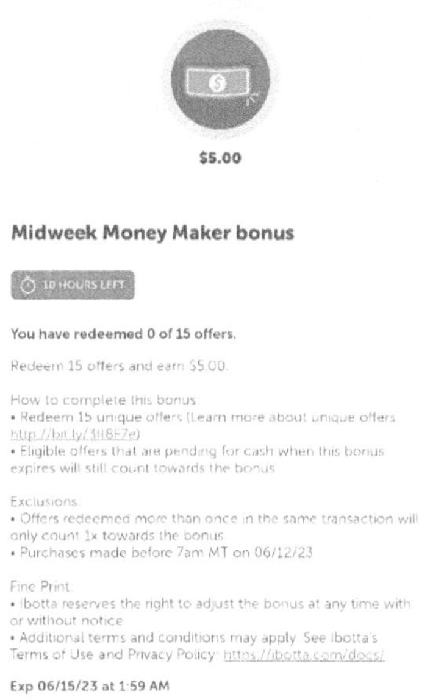

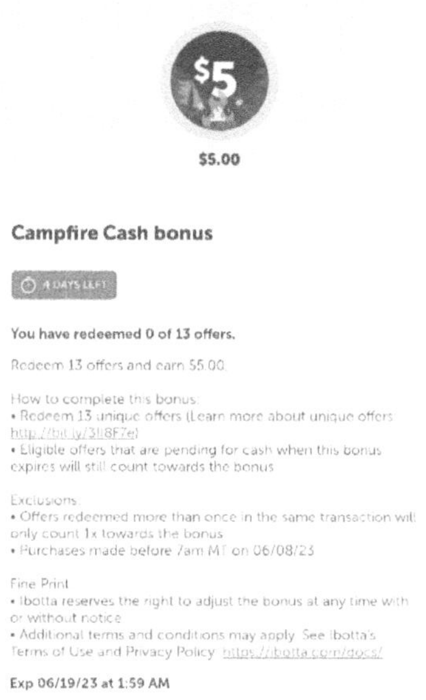

These amounts vary by account and only run from Monday to Wednesday, and a "Weekend Warrior" bonus runs from Thursday to Sunday. We must redeem fifteen offers to receive $5 back in this offer. This is in addition to all other offers we redeem and receive cash back for. The bonus on the right also gives back $5 for redeeming thirteen offers. These two bonuses will stack if you meet the one with the highest offers to redeem. If I redeem fifteen offers, I will receive $10 back for these bonuses and all the cash back for the offers I redeemed.

Once you have a minimum of $20 in your account, you can cash out to your PayPal or redeem the cash for digital gift cards. This is a great way to use rebate apps to pay for your couponing trips and continue to roll the deals each week never having to use your bank account to pay for couponing trips.

Fetch

Fetch is another awesome rebate app that is much simpler than Ibotta. Instead of giving cash back Fetch offers a point-based system; 1,000 points is equivalent to $1. They also have tons of products that gives points back for purchase.

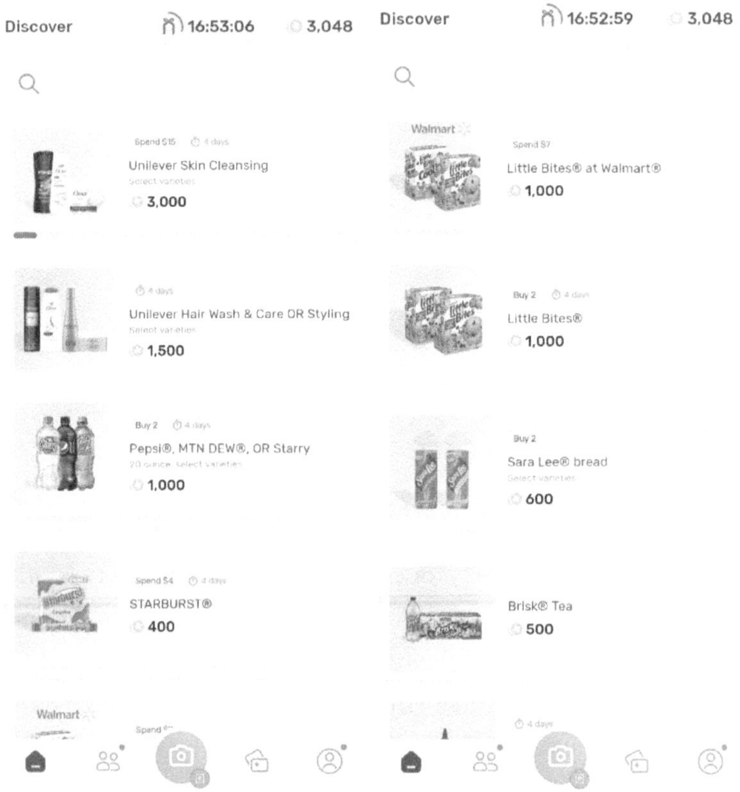

Most of these products are not store-specific, but some are, like the offer that says "Walmart" at the top. At the bottom, you will see a camera button. This allows you to scan your receipt and receive points. Once you receive a minimum of 5,000 points, you can redeem these points for digital gift cards to tons of different stores. Even stores you coupon at, such as CVS. These gift cards can also help to lower your out-of-pocket cost when couponing. This brings maximum savings, and with rebate apps, you will be amazed at how much money you save on things you buy weekly.

CONCLUSION

I pray that this book has given you the knowledge to coupon successfully. You can use this book as an instructional tool to help guide you until you build the confidence you need to be a successful couponer. My goal is to help you save money and relieve the pressure of inflation. You should have enough knowledge to be successful on your first couponing trip at whichever store you choose.

Blessings on your couponing journey!

Made in United States
Cleveland, OH
04 November 2026

47645126R00036